A TREASURY OF MARK TWAIN

The Wit and Wisdom
of a Great American Writer

*Edited by Edward Lewis
and Robert Myers*

Illustrated by James Parkinson

HALLMARK EDITIONS

A Treasury of Mark Twain

I have been an author for twenty-two years and an ass for fifty-five.

What a coward every man is! and how surely he will find it out if he will just let other people alone and sit down and examine himself. The human race is a race of cowards; and I am not only marching in that procession but carrying a banner.

This dream was like almost all the other dreams we indulge in in life, there was nothing in it.

The difference between the right word and the almost right word is the difference between lightning and the lightning bug.

Lying is universal — we *all* do it; we all *must* do it. Therefore, the wise thing is for us diligently to train ourselves to lie thoughtfully . . . .

Training is everything. The peach was once a bitter almond; cauliflower is nothing but cabbage with a college education.

There are people who strictly deprive themselves of each and every eatable, drinkable, and smokable which has in any way acquired a shady reputation. They pay this price for health. And health is all they get for it. How strange it is. It is like paying out your whole fortune for a cow that has gone dry.

I know the taste of the watermelon which has been honestly come by and I know the taste of the watermelon which has been acquired by art. Both taste good but the experienced know which tastes best.

Miss C. B. had her fine nose elegantly enameled, and the easy grace with which she blew it from time to time marked her as a cultivated and accomplished woman of the world; its exquisitely modulated tone excited the admiration of all who had the happiness to hear it.

It seems a pity that the world should throw away so many things merely because they are unwholesome. I doubt if God has given us any refreshment which, taken in moderation, is unwholesome, except microbes.

If you pick up a starving dog and make him prosperous, he will not bite you. This is the principle difference between a dog and a man.

A banker is a fellow who lends you his umbrella when the sun is shining and wants it back the minute it begins to rain.

Good little girls ought not to make mouths at their teachers for every trifling offence. This retaliation should only be resorted to under peculiarly aggravated circumstances.

There is no character, howsoever good and fine, but it can be destroyed by ridicule, howsoever poor and witless. Observe the ass, for instance: his character is about perfect, he is the choicest spirit among all the humbler animals, yet see what ridicule has brought him to. Instead of feeling complimented when we are called an ass, we are left in doubt.

I do not greatly mind being accused of a proclivity for rushing into print but at the same time I don't believe that the charge is really well founded. Suppose I did write eleven books, have you nothing to be grateful for? Go to — remember the forty-nine which I didn't write.

Everyone is a moon and has a dark side which he never shows to anybody.

Behold, the fool saith, "Put not all thine eggs in the one basket" — which is but a manner of saying, "Scatter your money and your attention"; but the wise man saith, "Put all your eggs in the one basket and — *WATCH THAT BASKET.*"

To worship rank and distinction is the dear and valued privilege of all the human race, and it is freely and joyfully exercised in democracies as well as in monarchies — and even, to some extent, among those creatures whom we impertinently call the Lower Animals. For even they have some poor little vanities and foibles, though in this matter they are paupers as compared to us.

The old saw says, "Let a sleeping dog lie." Right. Still, when there is much at stake it is better to get a newspaper to do it.

If I had a phrase-book of a really satisfactory sort I would study it, and not give all my free time to undictionarial readings, but there is no such work on the market. The existing phrase-books are inadequate. They are well enough as far as they go, but when you fall down and skin your leg they don't tell you what to say.

We should be careful to get out of an experience only the wisdom that is in it — and stop there; lest we be like the cat that sits down on a hot stove-lid. She will never sit down on a hot stove-lid again, and that is well; but also she will never sit down on a cold one any more.

It is often the case that the man who can't tell a lie thinks he is the best judge of one.

I reverently believe that the Maker who made us all makes everything in New England but the weather.

Beware of the struggling young author, my friends. Whom God sees fit to starve, let not man presumptuously rescue to his own undoing.

When she began to empty one of those sentences on me I unconsciously took the very attitude of reverence and stood uncovered, and if words had been water, I had been drowned sure.

Chambermaids are dead to every human instinct. If I can get a bill through the legislature abolishing chambermaids, I mean to do it.

The first notice that was taken of me when I "settled down" recently was by a gentleman who said he was an assessor, and connected with the U. S. Internal Revenue Department. I said I had never heard of his branch of business before, but I was very glad to see him all the same. Would he sit down? He sat down. I did not know anything particular to say, and yet I felt that people who have arrived at the dignity of keeping house must be conversational, must be easy and sociable in company. So, in default of anything else to say, I asked him if he was opening his shop in our neighborhood.

Animals talk to each other; I never knew but one man who could understand them — I knew he could because he told me so himself.

It is a good thing, perhaps, to write for the amusement of the public, but it is a far higher and nobler thing to write for their instruction, their profit, their actual and tangible benefit.

Wagner's music is better than it sounds.

To 'Young Author.' Yes, Agassiz does recommend authors to eat fish, because the phosphorus in it makes brain. So far you are correct. But I cannot help you to a decision about the amount you need to eat — at least, not with certainty. If the specimen composition you send is about your fair usual average, I should judge that perhaps a couple of whales would be all you would want for the present.

Why should we help the nation lie the whole day long and then object to telling one little individual private lie in our own interest to go to bed on? Just for the refreshment of it, I mean, and to take the rancid taste out of our mouth.

Of necessity, an Obituary is a thing which cannot be judiciously edited by any hand as by that of the subject of it.

All the human race loves a lord — that is, it loves to look upon or be noticed by the possessor of Power or Conspicuousness; and sometimes animals, born to better things and higher ideals, descend to man's level in this matter. In the *Jardin des Plantes* I have seen a cat that was so vain of being the personal friend of an elephant that I was ashamed of her.

He has been a doctor a year now and has had two patients — no, three, I think — yes, it was three; I attended their funerals.

These citizens of Flanders — Flounders, I think they call them, though I feel sure I have eaten a creature of that name or seen it in an aquarium or a menagerie, or in a picture or somewhere — are a thrifty, industrious race.

Science has recently discovered that the ant does not lay up anything for winter use. This will knock him out of literature, to some extent. He does not work, except when people are looking, and only then when the observer has a green, naturalistic look, and seems to be taking notes. This amounts to deception, and will injure him for the Sunday-schools.

Celebrating their landing! What was there remarkable about it, I would like to know? What can you be thinking of? Why, those Pilgrims had been at sea three or four months. It was the very middle of winter: it was as cold as death off Cape Cod there. Why shouldn't they come ashore? If they *hadn't* landed there would be some reason for celebrating the fact.

The truth is, a person's memory has no more sense than his conscience, and no appreciation whatever of values and proportions.

There is but one Homer, there is but one Shakespeare, there is but one McClintock — and his immortal book is before you.... It stands alone; it is monumental. It adds G. Ragsdale McClintock's to the sum of the republic's imperishable names.

Satan (impatiently) to Newcomer: The trouble with you Chicago people is that you think you are the best people down here, whereas you are merely the most numerous.

Courage is resistance to fear, mastery of fear — not absence of fear. Except a creature be part coward it is not a compliment to say it is brave; it is merely a loose misapplication of the word. Consider the flea! — incomparably the bravest of all the creatures of God, if ignorance of fear were courage. Whether you are asleep or awake he will attack you, caring nothing for the fact that in bulk and strength you are to him as are the massed armies of the earth to a sucking child; he lives both day and night and all days and nights in the very lap of peril and the immediate presence of death, and yet is no more afraid than is the man who walks the streets of a city that was threatened by an earthquake ten centuries before. When we speak of Clive, Nelson, and Putnam as men who "didn't know what fear was," we ought always to add the flea — and put him at the head of the procession.

Never run after your own hat — others will be delighted to do it; why spoil their fun?

Make it a point to do something every day that you don't want to do. This is the golden rule for acquiring the habit of doing your duty without pain.

If it please your neighbor to break the sacred calm of night with the snorting of an unholy trombone, it is your duty to put up with his wretched music and your privilege to pity him for the unhappy instinct that moves him to delight in such discordant sounds.

In the German it is true that by some oversight of the inventor of the language, a Woman is a female; but a Wife *(Weib)* is not — which is unfortunate. A Wife, here, has no sex; she is neuter; so, according to the grammar, a fish is *he,* his scales are *she,* but a fishwife is neither.

The first time I began to sneeze, a friend told me to go and bathe my feet in hot water and go to bed. I did so. Shortly afterward, another friend advised me to get up and take a cold shower-bath. I did that also. Within the hour, another friend assured me that it was policy to "feed a cold and starve a fever." I had both. So I thought it best to fill myself up for the cold, and then keep dark and let the fever starve awhile.

The first half of life consists of the capacity to enjoy without the chance; the last half consists of the chance without the capacity.

When a person has become seasoned by experience and has reached the age of sixty-four, which is the age of discretion, he likes a family compliment as well as ever, but he does not lose his head over it as in the old innocent days.

In San Francisco they used to claim that their native flea could kick a child over, as if it were a merit in a flea to be able to do that; as if the knowledge of it trumpeted abroad ought to entice immigration. Such a thing in nine cases out of ten would be almost sure to deter a thinking man from coming.

There was more Bull Run material scattered through the early camps of this country than exhibited itself at Bull Run. And yet it learned its trade presently and helped to fight the great battles later. I could have become a soldier myself if I had waited. I had got part of it learned, I knew more about retreating than the man that invented retreating.

There are many scapegoats for our sins, but the most popular is Providence.

"How deep is the well?"
"That, sir, I wit not, having never been told."
"How does the water usually stand in it?"
"Near to the top, these two centuries, as the testimony goeth, brought down to us through our predecessors."

There is no such thing as "the Queen's English." The property has gone into the hands of a joint stock company and we own the bulk of the shares.

The holy passion of Friendship is of so sweet and steady and loyal and enduring a nature that it will last through a whole lifetime, if not asked to lend money.

Whenever man makes a large stride in material prosperity and progress he is sure to think that *he* has progressed, whereas he has not advanced an inch, nothing has progressed but his circumstances. *He* stands where he stood before.

He was a very inferior farmer when he first began, but a prolonged and unflinching assault upon his agricultural difficulties has had its effect at last, and he is now fast rising from affluence to poverty.

Nothing helps scenery like ham and eggs.

There are eight hundred and sixty-nine different forms of lying, but only one of them has been squarely forbidden. Thou shalt not bear false witness against thy neighbor.

I think that all this courteous lying is a sweet and loving art, and should be cultivated. The highest perfection of politeness is only a beautiful edifice, built, from the base to the dome, of graceful and gilded forms of charitable and unselfish lying.

The efficiency of our criminal jury system is only marred by the difficulty of finding twelve men every day who don't know anything and can't read.

Without boasting, I think I may say I am not afraid to stand before a modern French duelist, but as long as I keep in my right mind I will never consent to stand behind one again.

its About wimins Rites. i Hev ReD A GUiD mANY LetteRs Rit bY wimin in YuR PAPeR, AnD I vow tHings is cummin to A oFFAL STAite when tHeY is AloUD to cARRi on At THem RAits. this cums of so mUCH sKooLin FoR GALS. tHeY wAnts to Be eQiL to us men.

My nerves had hardly grown quiet after this affair when they got another shake-up — one which utterly unmanned me for a moment: a rumor swept suddenly through the camp that one of the barkeepers had fallen over a precipice!

However, it turned out that it was only a chaplain.

Now I don't approve of dissipation, and I don't indulge in it, either; but I haven't a particle of confidence in a man who has no redeeming petty vices, and so I don't want to hear from you any more. I think you are the very same man who read me a long lecture last week about the degrading vice of smoking cigars, and then came back, in my absence, with your reprehensible fireproof gloves on, and carried off my beautiful parlor stove.

Hurry up and come to visit me before we get too old to hear each other swear.

James Peterson was the son of a common weaver, who was so miraculously poor that his friends were encouraged to believe that in case the Scriptures were carried out he would "inherit the earth." He never got his property.

If at any time you find it necessary to correct your brother, do not correct him with mud — never, on any account, throw mud at him, because it will spoil his clothes. It is better to scald him a little, for then you obtain desirable results. You secure his immediate attention to the lessons you are inculcating, and at the same time your hot water will have a tendency to remove impurities from his person, and possibly the skin, in spots.

"I have never spent such a half-hour in all my life before!" said I, with emotion; and I could have added, with a near approach to truth, "and I would rather be scalped than spend another one like it."

After a long immunity from the dreadful insanity that moves a man to become a musician in defiance of the will of God that he should confine himself to sawing wood, I finally fell a victim to the instrument they call the accordion. At this day I hate that contrivance as fervently as any man can, but at the time I speak of I suddenly acquired a disgusting and idolatrous affection for it. I got one of powerful capacity, and learned to play "Auld Lang Syne" on it. It seems to me, now, that I must have been gifted with a sort of inspiration to be enabled, in that state of ignorance in which I then was, to select out of the whole range of musical composition the one solitary tune that sounds vilest and most distressing on the accordion. I do not suppose there is another tune in the world with which I could have inflicted so much anguish upon my race as I did with that one during my short musical career.

"On with the dance, let joy be unconfined" is my motto, whether there's any dance to dance or any joy to unconfine.

Our Heavenly Father invented man because he was disappointed in the monkey.

Gratitude and treachery are merely the two extremities of the same procession. You have seen all of it that is worth staying for when the band and the gaudy officials have gone by.

It is more trouble to make a maxim than it is to do right.

There are people who can do all fine and heroic things but one: keep from telling their happiness to the unhappy.

Even the clearest and most perfect circumstantial evidence is likely to be at fault, after all, and therefore ought to be received with great caution. Take the case of any pencil sharpened by any woman: if you have witnesses you will find she did it with a knife, but if you take simply the aspect of the pencil you will say she did it with her teeth.

The English are mentioned in the Bible: *Blessed are the meek, for they shall inherit the earth.*

It would have been foolish to stand upon our dignity in a place where there was hardly room to stand upon our feet.

24

When I was a child I had to boil soap, notwith-standing my father was wealthy, and I had to get up early and study geometry at breakfast, and peddle my own poetry, and do everything just as Franklin did, in the solemn hope that I would be a Franklin some day. And here I am.

We have not all had the good fortune to be ladies. We have not all been generals, or poets, or statesmen; but when the toast works down to the babies, we stand on common ground.

Adam was but human — this explains it all. He did not want the apple for the apple's sake, he wanted it only because it was forbidden. The mistake was in not forbidding the serpent; then he would have eaten the serpent.

Do not undervalue the headache. While it is at its sharpest it seems a bad investment, but when relief begins the unexpired remainder is worth four dollars a minute.

In the first place God made idiots. This was for practice. Then He made School Boards.

I went often to look at the collection of curiosities in Heidelberg Castle, and one day I surprised the keeper of it with my German. I spoke entirely in that language. He was greatly interested; and after I had talked a while he said my German was very rare, possibly a "unique"; and wanted to add it to his museum.

If he had known what it had cost me to acquire my art, he would also have known that it would break any collector to buy it.

Yes, we do so love our little distinctions! And then we loftily scoff at a Prince for enjoying his larger ones; forgetting that if we only had his chance — ah!

You tell me whar a man gits his corn pone, en I'll tell you what his 'pinions is.

There isn't a Parallel of Latitude but thinks it would have been the Equator if it had had its rights.

When some men discharge an obligation you can hear the report for miles around.

Honest poverty is a gem that even a king might be proud to call his own, but I wish to sell out.

All that I care to know is that a man is a human being — that is enough for me; he can't be any worse.

There are those that believe that the most difficult thing to create is a woman who can comprehend that it is wrong to smuggle; and that an impossible thing to create is a woman who will not smuggle, whether or no, when she gets a chance. But these may be errors.

27

All infants appear to have an impertinent and disagreeable fashion nowadays of saying "smart" things on most occasions that offer, and especially on occasions when they ought not to be saying anything at all.

My own history would really seem so tame contrasted with that of my ancestors, that it is simply wisdom to leave it unwritten until I am hanged. If some other biographies I have read had stopped with the ancestry until a like event occurred, it would have been a felicitous thing for the reading public.

I hunted up another barometer; it was new and perfect. I boiled it half an hour in a pot of bean soup which the cooks were making. The result was unexpected: the instrument was not affected at all, but there was such a strong barometer taste to the soup that the head cook, who was a most conscientious person, changed its name in the bill of fare.

One cannot keep up a grudge against a vacuum.

There comes a time in every rightly constructed boy's life when he has a raging desire to go somewhere and dig for hidden treasure.

My parents were neither very poor nor conspicuously honest.

Whatever a man's age, he can reduce it several years by putting a bright-colored flower in his buttonhole.

Sufficient unto the day is one baby. As long as you are in your right mind don't you ever pray for twins. Twins amount to a permanent riot. And there ain't any real difference between triplets and an insurrection.

Familiarity breeds contempt — and children.

All religions issue Bibles against Satan, and say the most injurious things against him, but we never hear his side.

There are many humorous things in the world: among them the white man's notion that he is less savage than the other savages.

The emperor sent his troops to the field with immense enthusiasm; he will lead them in person — when they return.

History is better than prophecy. In fact history *is* prophecy. And history says that whenever a weak and ignorant people possess a thing which a strong and enlightened people want, it must be yielded up peaceably.

When one writes a novel about grown people, he knows exactly where to stop — that is, with a marriage; but when he writes of juveniles, he must stop where he best can.

A crime persevered in a thousand centuries ceases to be a crime and becomes a virtue.

The way it is now, the asylums can hold the sane people, but if we tried to shut up the insane we should run out of building materials.

The surest way to disturb the center of gravity is by the skillful employment of a good joke.

I prefer pure water.... I therefore commenced, several years ago, to devise ways and means to purify the Buffalo River water supplied to the city, and I have succeeded to perfection. I have raised to perfection a splendid moustache that acts as the most complete filter ever invented.

31

I believe that whenever a human being, of even the highest intelligence and culture, delivers an opinion upon a matter apart from his particular and especial line of interest, training, and experience, it will always be an opinion of so foolish and so valueless a sort that it can be depended upon to suggest to our Heavenly Father that the human being is another disappointment, and that he is no considerable improvement upon the monkey.

We were in bed by ten, for we wanted to be up and away on our tramp homeward with the dawn. I hung fire, but Harris went to sleep at once. I hate a man who goes to sleep at once; there is a sort of indefinable something about it which is not exactly an insult, and yet is an insolence; and one which is hard to bear, too.

A man delivers a single brutal "Goodbye," and that is the end of it. Not so with the gentle sex — I say it in their praise; they cannot abide abruptness.

Consider that conversation by telephone — when you are simply sitting by and not taking any part in that conversation — is one of the solemnest curiosities of this modern life.

There's always something about your success that displeases even your best friends.

I do not remember my first lie, it is too far back.

How easy it is to make people believe a lie, and how hard it is to undo that work again!

Always do right; this will gratify some people and astonish the rest.

Wrinkles should merely indicate where smiles have been.

It is our nature to conform; it is a force which not many can successfully resist. What is its seat? The inborn requirement of self-approval.

Sentimental young folks still take stock in that beautiful old saying that when the baby smiles in his sleep, it is because the angels are whispering to him. Very pretty, but too thin — simply wind on the stomach, my friends.

I was born without teeth — and there Richard III had the advantage of me; but I was born without a humpback, likewise, and there I had the advantage of him.

When I speak my native tongue in its utmost purity in England, an Englishman can't understand me at all.

One mustn't criticize other people on grounds where he can't stand perpendicular himself.

Men think they think upon great political questions, and they do; but they think with their party, not independently; they read its literature but not that of the other side; they arrive at convictions but they are drawn from a partial view of the matter in hand and are of no particular value.

A man must and will have his own approval first of all, in each and every moment and circumstance of his life — even if he must repent of a self-approved act the moment after its commission in order to get his self-approval *again.*

I have long ago lost belief in immortality — also my interest in it.

If you wish to lower yourself in a person's favor, one good way is to tell his story over again, the way *you* heard it.

34

Good breeding consists in concealing how much we think of ourselves and how little we think of the other person.

She asked me not to gamble. She whispered and said, "Put up those wicked cards this minute! — two pair and a jack, you numskull, and the other fellow's got a flush!"

What I bemoan is the growing prevalence of the brutal truth. Let us do what we can to eradicate it. An injurious truth has no merit over an injurious lie. Neither should ever be uttered.

I like criticism, but it must be my way.

Man was made at the end of the week's work when God was tired.

To cease smoking is the easiest thing I ever did; I ought to know because I've done it a thousand times.

Tell the truth or trump — but get the trick.

I used to worship the mighty genius of Michelangelo — that man who was great in poetry, painting, sculpture, architecture — great in everything he undertook. But I do not want Michelangelo for breakfast — for luncheon — for dinner — for tea — for supper — for between meals. I like a change occasionally. In Genoa, he designed everything; in Milan he or his pupils designed everything; he designed the Lake of Como..., in Florence, he painted everything.... In Pisa he designed everything but the old shot-tower, and they would have at-

36

tributed that to him if it had not been so aw-
fully out of the perpendicular....

I never felt so fervently thankful, so soothed,
so tranquil, so filled with a blessed peace, as I
did yesterday when I learned that Michelangelo
was dead.

It is not worth while to try to keep history from
repeating itself, for man's character will always
make the preventing of the repetitions impossible.

There is no end to the laws, and no beginning
to the execution of them.

What is your Aim in Life? — To endeavor to
be absent when my time comes.
What is your Motto? — Be virtuous and you
will be eccentric.

Part of the secret of success in life is to eat what
you like and let the food fight it out inside.

Few slanders can stand the wear of silence.

It is curious — curious that physical courage
should be so common in the world and moral
courage so rare.

Celebrity is what a boy or a youth longs for more than for any other thing. He would be a clown in a circus, he would be a pirate, he would sell himself to Satan, in order to attract attention and be talked about and envied.

The reports of my death are greatly exaggerated.

Even the average child should know better. It should know that any strange and much-talked-of event is always followed by imitations, the world being so well supplied with excitable people who only need a little stirring up to make them lose what is left of their heads and do mad things which they would not have thought of ordinarily.

It is your human environment that makes climate.

Any mummery will cure if the patient's faith is strong in it.

There is a Moral Sense and there is an Immoral Sense. History shows us that the Moral Sense enables us to perceive morality and how to avoid it, and that the Immoral Sense enables us to perceive immorality and how to enjoy it.

When people do not respect us we are sharply offended; yet deep down in his private heart no man much respects himself.

Whenever the literary German dives into a sentence, that is the last you are going to see of him till he emerges on the other side of his Atlantic with his verb in his mouth.

Yes, it is strange how little a while at a time a person can be contented.

Loyalty to petrified opinion never yet broke a chain or freed a human soul.

A crowd was as bad for a magician's miracle in that day as it was for a spiritualist's miracle in mine; there was sure to be some skeptic on hand to turn up the gas at the crucial moment and spoil everything.

We all do no end of feeling and we mistake it for thinking. And out of it we get an aggregation which we consider a boon. Its name is Public Opinion. It is held in reverence. It settles everything. Some think it the Voice of God.

I talked with her with daring frankness, frequently calling a spade a spade instead of coldly symbolizing it as a snow shovel; and on her side she was equally frank. It was one of the damnedest conversations I have ever had with a beautiful stranger of her sex, if I do say it myself that shouldn't.

One should always "get even" in some way, else the sore place will go on hurting.

It could probably be shown by facts and figures that there is no distinctly native American criminal class except Congress.

The man with a new idea is a Crank until the idea succeeds.

Hunger is the handmaid of genius.

When a person of mature age perpetrates a practical joke it is fair evidence, I think, that he is weak in the head and hasn't enough heart to signify.

Unquestionably, the popular thing in this world is novelty.

You can't throw too much style into a miracle.

I am an old man and have known a great many troubles, but most of them never happened.

Whoever has lived long enough to find out what life is, knows how deep a debt of gratitude we owe to Adam, the first great benefactor of our race. He brought death into the world.

The very ink with which all history is written is merely fluid prejudice.

In statesmanship get the formalities right, never mind about the moralities.

Even popularity can be overdone. In Rome, along at first, you are full of regrets that Michelangelo died, but by and by you only regret that you didn't see him do it.

It is easy to find fault, if one has that disposition. There was once a man who, not being able to find any other fault with his coal, complained that there were too many prehistoric toads in it.

Nothing so needs reforming as other people's habits.

April 1. This is the day upon which we are reminded of what we are on the other three hundred and sixty-four.

Noise proves nothing. Often a hen who has merely laid an egg cackles as if she had laid an asteroid.

There is no school in all our land where the young ladies do not feel obliged to close their compositions with a sermon; and you will find that the sermon of the most frivolous and the least religious girl in the school is always the longest and the most relentlessly pious.

It is by the goodness of God that in our country we have those three unspeakably precious things: freedom of speech, freedom of conscience, and the prudence never to practice either of them.

Let us endeavor so to live that when we come to die even the undertaker will be sorry.

Be careless in your dress if you must but keep a tidy soul.

By trying we can easily learn to endure adversity. Another man's, I mean.

Grief can take care of itself; but to get the full value of a joy you must have somebody to divide it with.

When in doubt, tell the truth.

The true Southern watermelon is a boon apart and not to be mentioned with commoner things. It is chief of this world's luxuries, king by the grace of God over all the fruits of the earth. When one has tasted it, he knows what the angels eat. It was not a Southern watermelon that Eve took; we know it because she repented.

Nature makes the locust with an appetite for crops; man would have made him with an appetite for sand.

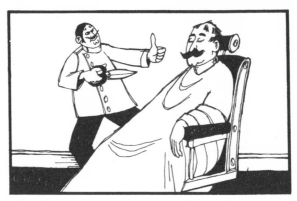

All things change except barbers, the ways of barbers, and the surroundings of barbers. These never change. What one experiences in a barber's shop the first time he enters one is what he always experiences in barbers' shops afterward till the end of his days.

I do no violence to the usual license of history by inferring that Noah liked hog, for he named one of his sons Ham.

Let us be grateful to Adam our benefactor. He cut us out of the "blessing" of idleness and won for us the "curse" of labor.

Thanksgiving Day. Let all give humble, hearty, and sincere thanks, now, but the turkeys. In the island of Fiji they do not use turkeys; they use plumbers. It does not become you and me to sneer at Fiji.

To be good is noble, but to teach others how to be good is nobler — and less trouble.

Water, taken in moderation, cannot hurt anybody.

What a good thing Adam had — when he said a good thing, he knew nobody had said it before.

We can secure other people's approval if we do right and try hard, but our own is worth a hundred of it and no way has been found out of securing that.

The man who is ostentatious of his modesty is twin to the statue that wears a fig-leaf.

He had had much experience of physicians, and said "the only way to keep your health is to eat what you don't want, drink what you don't like, and do what you'd druther not."

When your watch gets out of order you have a choice of two things to do: throw it in the fire or take it to the watch-tinker. The former is the quickest.

I've never heard a blue jay use bad grammar, but very seldom; and when they do, they are as ashamed as a human.

There are several good protections against temptations but the surest is cowardice.

Man will do many things to get himself loved, he will do all things to get himself envied.

When a man's dog turns against him it is time for a wife to pack her trunk and go home to mama.

46

It takes your enemy and your friend, working together, to hurt you to the heart, the one to slander you and the other to get the news to you.

Often, the surest way to convey misinformation is to tell the strict truth.

The country is the real thing, the substantial thing, the eternal thing; it is the thing to watch over and care for and be loyal to; institutions are extraneous, they are its mere clothing, and clothing can wear out, become ragged, cease to be comfortable, cease to protect the body from winter, disease, and death.

When you cannot get a compliment in any other way, pay yourself one.

Woman is unrivaled as a wet nurse.

Often, the less there is to justify a traditional custom, the harder it is to get rid of it.

He liked words — big words, fine words, grand words, rumbling, thundering, reverberating words; with sense attached if it could be got in without marring the sound, but not otherwise.

47

The man who tells a lie to help a poor devil out of trouble is one of whom the angels doubtless say, "Lo, here is an heroic soul who casts his own welfare into jeopardy to succor his neighbor's; let us exalt this magnanimous liar."

Everybody was sorry she died; but I reckoned with her disposition — she was having a better time in the graveyard.

I could never learn to like her — except on a raft at sea with no other provisions in sight.

Most writers regard truth as their most valuable possession, and therefore are most economical in its use.

Some of the commonest English words are not in use with us — such as 'ousemaid, 'ospital, 'otel, 'istorian.

When I was two years of age she asked me not to drink, and then I made a resolution of total abstinence. That I have adhered to it and enjoyed the beneficent effects of it through all time, I owe to my grandmother. I have never drunk a drop from that day to this of any kind of water.

My mother had a great deal of trouble with me but I think she enjoyed it.

'Classic.' A book which people praise and don't read.

The human race was always interesting and we know by its past that it will always continue so. Monotonously.

Every man is a master and also a servant, a vassal. There is always someone who looks up to him and admires and envies him; there is always someone to whom he looks up and whom he admires and envies. This is his nature; this is his character.

The timid man yearns for full value and demands a tenth. The bold man strikes for double value and compromises on par.

Ignorant people think it's the noise which fight-
ing cats make that is so aggravating, but it ain't
so; it's the sickening grammar they use.

There is no use in your walking five miles to
fish when you can depend on being just as un-
successful near home.

Arguments have no chance against petrified
training; they wear it as little as the waves wear
a cliff.

It usually takes me more than three weeks to
prepare a good impromptu speech.

The man who is a pessimist before forty-eight
knows too much; the man who is an optimist
after forty-eight knows too little.

When I reflect upon the number of disagreeable people who I know have gone to a better world, I am moved to lead a different life.

Habit is habit and not to be flung out of the window by any man but coaxed downstairs a step at a time.

Why is it that we rejoice at a birth and grieve at a funeral? It is because we are not the person involved.

Virtue has never been as respectable as money.

Live hog can only be restrained by a stout pen; but in some communities you cannot be sure of preventing the straying of dead hog by any precaution.

There ain't no way to find out why a snorer can't hear himself snore.

We do not deal much in facts when we are contemplating ourselves.

I can't do no literary work for the rest of this year because I'm meditating another lawsuit and looking around for a defendant.

51

The habits of all peoples are determined by their circumstances. The Bermudians lean upon barrels because of the scarcity of lampposts.

The Creator made Italy from designs by Michelangelo.

It were not best that we should all think alike; it is difference of opinion that makes horse-races.

Truth is stranger than Fiction, but it is because Fiction is obliged to stick to possibilities; Truth isn't.

Man is the only animal that blushes. Or needs to.

To succeed in the other trades, capacity must be shown; in the law, concealment of it will do.

If the desire to kill and the opportunity to kill came always together, who would escape hanging?

It has always been my rule never to smoke when asleep, and never to refrain when awake.

Simple rules for saving money: To save half, when you are fired by an eager impulse to contribute to a charity, wait and count forty. To save three-quarters, count sixty. To save it all, count sixty-five.

Be good and you will be lonesome.

Few things are harder to put up with than the annoyance of a good example.

She was not quite what you would call refined. She was not quite what you would call unrefined. She was the kind of person that keeps a parrot.

Heaven goes by favor; if it went by merit, you would stay out and your dog would go in.

Don't part with your illusions. When they are gone you may still exist but you have ceased to live.

It was wonderful to find America, but it would have been more wonderful to miss it.

To eat is human; to digest, divine.

Much as the modern French duel is ridiculed by certain smart people, it is in reality one of the most dangerous institutions of our day. Since it is always fought in the open air, the combatants are nearly sure to catch cold.

Consider well the proportions of things. It is better to be a young June-bug than an old bird of paradise.

What is the difference between a taxidermist and a tax collector? The taxidermist takes only your skin.

Let us be thankful for the fools. But for them the rest of us could not succeed.

Nothing could divert them from the regular and faithful performance of the pieties enjoined by the Church. More than once I had seen a noble who had gotten his enemy at a disadvantage stop to pray before cutting his throat.

It used to be a good hotel, but that proves nothing — I used to be a good boy.

A man is accepted into a church for what he believes and he is turned out for what he knows.

The Autocrat of Russia possesses more power than any other man in the earth, but he cannot stop a sneeze.

If you tell the truth, you don't have to remember anything.

It is not best that we use our morals week-days; it gets them out of repair for Sundays.

Let us not be too particular; it is better to have old secondhand diamonds than none at all.

There are those who scoff at the school-boy, calling him frivolous and shallow, yet it was the school-boy who said, "Faith is believing what you know ain't so."

Truth is the most valuable thing we have. Let us economize it.

All say, "How hard it is that we have to die"—a strange complaint to come from the mouths of people who have had to live.

More than one cigar at a time is excessive smoking.

I am sorry to be vain — at least I am sorry to expose the fact that I am vain — but I do confess it and expose it.

In all matters of opinion, our adversaries are insane.

There is an old-time toast which is golden for its beauty, "When you ascend the hill of prosperity may you not meet a friend."

Barring that natural expression of villainy which we all have, the man looked honest enough.

I have never let my schooling interfere with my education.

Pity is for the living, envy is for the dead.

There is a lot to say in her favor, but the other is more interesting.

Reader, suppose you were an idiot; and suppose you were a member of Congress; but I repeat myself.

The older we grow the greater becomes our wonder at how much ignorance one can contain without bursting one's clothes.

There are two times in a man's life when he should not speculate: when he can't afford it and when he can.

Soap and education are not as sudden as a massacre, but they are more deadly in the long run.

One of the most striking differences between a cat and a lie is that a cat has only nine lives.

The chief dish was the renowned fish called pompano, delicious as the less criminal forms of sin.

There are no people who are quite so vulgar as the overrefined ones.

Repartee is something we think of twenty-four hours too late.

A wise man does not waste so good a commodity as lying for naught.

Fleas can be taught nearly anything that a Congressman can.

He is useless on top of the ground; he ought to be under it, inspiring the cabbages.

There were some that believed he would be President yet, if he escaped hanging.

Only presidents, editors, and people with tapeworms have the right to use the editorial "we."

The spirit of wrath — not the words — is the sin; and the spirit of wrath is cursing. We begin to swear before we can talk.

His money is twice tainted: 'taint yours and 'taint mine.

All you need in this life is ignorance and confidence, and then success is sure.

Adam and Eve had many advantages, but the principal one was that they escaped teething.

Each person is born to one possession which outvalues all his others — his last breath.

Church ain't shucks to a circus.

He was an old numskull, a magician who believed in his own magic, and no magician can thrive who is handicapped with a superstition like that.

I can live for two months on a good compliment.

I don't give a damn for a man that can spell a word only one way.

It is easier to stay out than get out.

Prosperity is the best protector of principle.

A Treasury of Mark Twain

Designed by Harald Peter.
Set in photocomposed Times Roman,
designed in 1931 for The London Times.
Printed on Hallmark Eggshell Book paper.